Commercial Diving

Discover How to Become a Commercial Diver

~ Insight into the World of Commercial Diving ~

by Scott Williams

Table of Contents

Introduction

It's nice to be able to tell people that you're a commercial diver. It's an exciting profession, one that's both physically and mentally demanding, somehow capable of simultaneously being "hands-on" and also intensely cerebral. The substantial amount of money you can make is great too, especially considering how quickly you can be trained.

Another nice thing about being a commercial diver is that the profession is expansive and growing. There are commercial divers employed as marine photojournalists, others work for the police department, scouring river bottoms for missing persons. There are specialized divers trained to handle sensitive jobs around hazardous or even nuclear sites. Perhaps the largest employer of commercial divers is the offshore oil rig industry, which employs commercial divers as underwater welders and repairmen who live on the rig for days at a time. Although the work may not be as "steady" as a typical job since it's often seasonal and you may work on a contract-by-contract basis based on project availability, the field is steadily growing at a rate that significantly outpaces the average growth rate of other professions.

This book is designed to provide a comprehensive, detailed, step-by-step guide for individuals interested in pursuing the commercial diving profession. If you want to learn all about what the commercial diving has to offer you, and how you can become a commercial diver, then read on.

Chapter 1: Getting a Dive Physical

Even occasional recreational diving can be demanding on the body. Commercial divers will be diving on a very regular basis, often at depths that recreational divers wouldn't normally touch. It's important for aspiring commercial divers to be in good physical condition. This is not to say that only Olympic athletes can attempt entry into this profession, but well-rounded personal fitness will go a long way towards ensuring your success as a diver. Employers who hire commercial divers require a diving physical that's been completed within the last three years. For divers over 40, the physical will need to be completed within the last two years. You can expect the commercial diving physical to be much more comprehensive than a standard physical examination.

On the Association of Diving Contractors International website—www.adc-int.org—you can download a diver medical form. Should you require a diving physical, take this form to any licensed physician and ask for the checkup to be done.

The diving physical is quite comprehensive, and there are a multitude of factors which could potentially disqualify would-be commercial divers. Pulmonary and cardiovascular conditions will be looked at very closely. Divers can be disqualified for asthma, breathing disorders, or cardiovascular disorders, among other things. Other random factors will also be considered, such as any deformities of the body that would prevent you from being able to wear the required diving equipment. For example, if your mouth is misshaped to a point where it's impossible for you to wear the required diving mouthpiece, then you could be disqualified. In general, you must be in good physical condition with no liability that would make it unsafe for you to dive on a regular basis. Prospective divers are also subject to a series of lab tests, x-rays, and strength tests. If you satisfy all requirements, the physician will certify you as "fit for diving" on the diver medical form.

In addition to demonstrating physical wellness, hopeful commercial divers should also be psychologically healthy. The ability to work and think under pressure and to manage stress is critical in this profession. Drug testing, initially during the physical, and on a regular basis, is a norm in the commercial diving world.

Many diving schools have a resident or go-to physician that can administer diving physicals for incoming students. You'll likely incur a charge of a couple hundred dollars for their services.

Chapter 2: Selecting a School

In order to be certified by the Association of Diving Contractors International, you must have a high school diploma or the equivalent. It's also helpful if you have higher aptitudes in mathematics, engineering, and a basic understanding of how to use common tools. The biggest hump you'll need to get over will take you less than a year to complete—you must complete 625 hours of formal training. These hours are obtained by enrolling in one of several commercial diving schools throughout the world. To find a list of accredited programs, go to the ADCI website—www.adc-int.org—and on the "membership directory" page, select "school" from the "Member Type" drop down menu. Click submit search and you'll get a listing of all the certified schools in the world.

How Much Does It Cost?

The most basic certification available "entry level tender/diver" will cost approximately eight thousand dollars and will require about two months to complete. More sophisticated programs take four to twelve months and will cost between fifteen and twenty thousand dollars. You will also be able to find schools that offer commercial diving in affiliation with local community colleges as a part of an accredited two-year program, such as the Marine Technology Program at Santa Barbara City College in Santa Barbara, California. If you're fortunate enough to live near a community college that offers a commercial diving curriculum, then you may be able to take advantage of the college's standard financial aid opportunities to help finance your education.

Most commercial diving schools can be paid for with various forms of financial aid, such as Pell Grants, GI Bill, Unsubsidized and Subsidized Stafford loans, as well as state-based vocational rehabilitation funding. Several institutes also have working partnerships with major banks such as Wells Fargo, Sallie Mae, and Regions Bank to provide private funding. If you need a private loan, but don't have great credit or any assets, you have the option of obtaining your loan with the help of a co-signer.

Is Age a Factor?

Though there are students who become certified in commercial diving well into their 50s, age, realistically, is a factor that's taken into account in the commercial diving industry. After a person surpasses his mid-forties, he's more vulnerable to the risks associated with commercial diving and is thus less likely to be hired.

What to Prepare for

Diving school is a mix of classroom and hands-on activities. Some schools have an orientation tank that students use for about four weeks before going on to open water, and eventually deep water dives. In the practice tank, you'll learn the basics of how to use the valves on your dive helmet and how to know when to use surface air and when to use your local bailout tank.

Once you're doing open water dives, you'll begin to learn more about welding, both on land and underwater. You'll also learn all about Ultra-Thermic burning, which, if you've seen any ads for diving schools, you'll notice how they love to feature this exciting practice of using extremely high temperatures (10,000 degrees Fahrenheit) to burn away virtually anything, even in fully submerged water. The deep diving section is probably the most challenging aspect of the curriculum, and some students will inevitably struggle here. Not only will you have to competently deal with high pressure, but deep dives also come with big visibility challenges and can be very muddy, making it hard to see and maneuver.

Students learn diving safety front to back: all about decompression, human physiology while diving, the physics of diving, as well as the use and safe handling of underwater explosives and rigging.

School Selection

If you're able to relocate, then don't limit yourself to the diving school that's closest to where you live; try to enroll in the school that is, in your estimation, the most appealing. Especially if you are pursuing a highly specialized curriculum such as welding, hazard diving, or nuclear diving, you want the training that's the best fit. Good diving schools will also make available the statistics which show the gainful employment of their graduates, so be sure to look over these as well.

You'll find that commercial diving schools fall broadly into two categories, the private trade schools—these are the schools that usually advertise more often and offer curriculums that are shorter in duration—and the public college programs, which are normally longer in duration, but with more expansive options for financial aid. If you're approaching commercial diving with an already established background in trade skills, you'll probably fare better in one of the private schools with the more compact curriculum timelines.

The Internet is great, but don't underestimate the usefulness of an old-fashioned on-site visit to the schools you're interested in. Make a little vacation out of it. For example, if you're a Midwesterner interested in diving, then scouting diving schools are a great excuse to tour the west coast. When you visit a school, try to get an interview with a faculty member. An administrator will be able to fill you in on all the facts surrounding the school's curriculum, the time required to get certified, and the cost, but the faculty members are the persons whom you'll be seeing and working with on an ongoing basis. It's important that you have good chemistry with your future teachers. It's also important that you have good chemistry with your fellow classmates, so find one or two students to sit down with for lunch and an informal chat. Find out what they like best and least about the program, what the major challenges are and how bright the job prospects post certification are. While visiting, you should also, of course, check out the premises of the campus and the condition of the equipment and facilities. If permitted, try to sit in on a class and feel out what the classroom environment will look and feel like. Don't just appear in class unannounced; arrange your classroom sit-in with an instructor or an administrator.

Another way to feel out a school is by contacting a handful of commercial diving companies and speaking with someone who hires or recruits divers (usually the operations manager). Ask her how she feels about the schools you're considering and how many graduates are regularly hired out of that school. When interfacing with commercial diving companies, be sure to be polite, announce your intentions up front and thank them for their time. If you leave a good impression, then they'll be more likely to favorably remember you in a few months' time when you're scouring the job market for your first commercial diving gig.

Another, and perhaps the most important, critical assessment you must make is of yourself and the skills you're bringing to the table as you begin your training as a commercial diver. For instance, if you have extensive mechanical knowledge, or if you've already trained or been certified as a welder, then your main objective in commercial diving school is to understand the ins and outs as well as ups and downs of diving itself. Your mechanical skills will readily translate into your new curriculum and provide you with a significant advantage. If you have no mechanical skills whatsoever, you're better off choosing a school that has welding and rigging emphasized early and often in the curriculum. Another idea would be to train on some of the adjunct mechanical skills prior to attending diving school.

If you're a seasoned recreational diver, then you should look for programs that offer a shorter path towards certification, under the assumption that the curriculum will be compressed and will move along at a quicker pace.

Chapter 3: Getting the Most Out of Training

The people that end up being the most successful commercial divers are those who take pride in their work from the very early stages. Regardless of your skill level, this attitude is essential to have if you want to thrive during and after diving school. You're not just competing with other students, you're also competing with yourself, doing everything you can to develop the skills you need to become a great commercial diver.

When it comes to being a good student, there's, of course, the basic stuff—pay attention, get plenty of sleep, study hard and so on. But in commercial diving, the stakes are even higher than in most types of vocational trainings. The skills you learn at school are the skills you will need to stay safe while doing your job. They could save your life one day.

Another thing to consider is that the better students are more likely to get recommendations from their teachers when the time comes to enter the fray of job hunting. Fortunately, there are a lot of jobs in commercial diving, so the competition won't be cutthroat, but if you want to get the best paying jobs after you complete your training, then you should strive to fully engage in your academic curriculum.

If you're not the best classroom student in general, you can make up for it by getting really good at the hands-on material. Again, taking pride in your work is key. Also, if you feel that a lot is going over your head in the classroom, don't succumb to thinking that everyone else totally gets it. Odds are, if something confuses you, then it's probably confusing to everyone else as well.

Put Some Pressure on Yourself and Keep Your Eyes on the Prize

No pun intended, but for an aspiring commercial diver, a little pressure is a good thing. Even though most people are able to get through their training and certification, there are definitely those that don't know how to parlay their new skill set into a good job. During your time as a student, it's critical that you

20

investigate opportunities and learn about the industry as much as possible. Always take advantage of opportunities to meet with faculty members to discuss career paths. This is the easiest way to set yourself apart from the crowd. Faculty member will be more enthusiastic recommending someone who is enthusiastic about finding a great job.

If you're feeling reluctant about committing the time and money to go to school, then consider first training in a slightly more broad area such as welding or carpentry and pursuing the diving component at a later time. This way you'll have a broader job market available to you in the long run.

Chapter 4: Scoring Your First Job

A Job Hunt Is a Job

Many recently certified commercial divers make the mistake of thinking a job will be served up to them on a silver platter after they've been certified. Unfortunately, just as in any other schooling or training program, finishing your studies simply puts you in the hunt. It doesn't guarantee you anything.

The tricky thing about the job hunt is that, in order to be successful, you have to treat it as a job in and of itself, just without the time cards and without a boss holding you accountable, and, worst of all, without the paycheck. Not easy for some, impossible for others. Think of it this way, if you had the discipline to get through school, then you should also be able to summon enough discipline to execute a good job hunt. You need to put in eight hours a day at least and work really hard. Get your resume in top condition, apply, follow-up, and work your network. Your efforts will pay off.

You should also be open to taking additional technical courses that will make your candidacy more attractive to employers. Commercial diving companies are becoming more and more high-tech and being able to offer a few additional technical capacities is a great way to stand out from the crowd.

If you have some basic Excel knowledge, then keep a running spreadsheet of everywhere you've applied and whom you spoke with, and schedule an appropriate follow-up by phone or email. Even if you aren't comfortable with Excel (and don't have a friend, girlfriend, boyfriend or spouse to assist you), you can still keep your job search organized with a basic notepad. You may also uncover information about your prospective employers such as the key technical skills they're looking for. This can be found out by making direct phone or email contact, and it can also be learned by doing research on the Internet. See if you can identify what they need by reviewing the types of jobs being posted. How can you position yourself as the ideal candidate to meet their stated needs?

Keep your fellow students close with social media. They may be able to tip you off if a company is doing a big round of hiring. If you're trying to find out information on a specific company, use LinkedIn (you'll have to set up an account) and post a question. People will respond.

The most critical tip to remember during your job search is to not give up. Giving up is what prevents most people from finding success. They see a mountain of debt to pay back, they get spooked and end up falling back on a non-diving job and ultimately earning less than they would have made had they continued looking for work as a commercial diver. Get up every day (at least five days a week) and put in your work on the job hunt. Something will break loose for you eventually.

Another popular decompression procedural aid used by commercial divers is known as "saturation diving." This procedure involves the diver living in pressurized chambers for long periods of time, so much so that they become completely saturated by the inert gas used in their breathing mixture, which is usually helium. Once saturated, the diver's decompression time will always be the same regardless of circumstances.

Thanks to commercial divers and companies with know-how on matters of decompression, decompression sickness is no longer as problematic or prevalent as it was in the past. In fact, most governments mandate the presence of a decompression chamber on commercial diving job sites.

Despite our more sophisticated methods and technologies, divers will inevitably encounter decompression sickness at some point or another during their careers. If you report your symptoms promptly and get the treatment you need, then you should recover fully from decompression sickness. The best way to prevent and minimize bouts of decompression sickness is by learning everything there is to know about the proper use of decompression chambers.

Chapter 6: Staying Warm

Since the work of a commercial diver is hard enough as is, most commercial diving companies will do all they can to ensure there divers remain as comfortable as possible while working. Heat can be a really big factor. It's very unpleasant doing hard work while you're freezing cold, just ask the oil field workers in Alberta, Canada.

For shallow dives, wet suits can be adequate as a heating source, but when a diver is immersing himself in temperatures colder than 60 to 65 degrees Fahrenheit for a prolonged period of time, then other heating measures must be considered.

Dry suits and hot water suits are two of the most common suits used for added warmth. Dry suits are also known as "passive thermal protection." They have no external heating source but instead rely on trapping the diver's body heat. If helium is being used in the tank as a component of the mixed-gas, then dry suits are not going to be the best solution. Helium directs heat away from the body, cooling it down from the inside out and essentially counter-acting the efficacy of the dry suit. Another problem with dry suits is that they completely cease to be effective if they get punctured, and seeing as the job of a commercial diver is an industrial job, there is a chance that the suit could get torn or punctured at some point. If the diver is at a very low depth and must go through several minutes worth of decompression before surfacing, then a compromised dry suit could result in an extended and possibly dangerous period of cold.

Hot water suits are generally regarded as better options for providing heat. The hot water system contains a topside heat source, such a diesel-fired burner or steam unit. Using a pump, hot water is circulated to the diver's vicinity. This mechanism is especially well suited to commercial divers who perform stationary work such as underwater photography.

Chapter 7: Staying Healthy

In addition to decompression sickness, there are a variety of other maladies that may affect the commercial diver, especially during saturation dives in which the body will be exposed both to high pressures and isolated living environments for extended periods of time.

Among the potential health hazards of saturation diving is High Pressure Nervous Syndrome (HPNS), which can create feelings of nausea, drowsiness, and loss of appetite. The symptoms will usually develop in the early phases of the saturation dive and will normally subside after the diver's been down at the target depth for a while. The major problem with HPNS is that it's unclear what exactly causes these symptoms, and if you're caught off guard with a bout of HPNS while you're working, then the consequences could be disastrous.

Another common malady that will gradually wear away on saturation divers is aseptic bone necrosis which is the wearing away of the heads of the bodies longest bones, such as the top most part of the arm or leg bone. This condition develops over time and the worst-case scenario is the development of a chronic joint aching similar to arthritis.

Cleanliness is of exceptional importance while on a saturation dive, because, since you're in an isolated environment, a fungal infection can rapidly become severe. There's more of a risk of developing a fungal infection during your saturations dive if you're diving in hotter and humid waters and if cleanliness is a problem. Humid conditions are also apt to result in ear infections. Divers typically use prophylactics to ward off ear infections, but they can never be totally immune. Cleanliness will also help prevent the spread of contagious disease within a saturation dive. In at least one case, a hepatitis infection was spread from one diver to another due to an unclean saturation system.

Chapter 8: Staying Safe

Commercial diving is often thought of as a daring, adventurous profession that carries with it a large amount of risk. In truth, it's impossible to quantify in any meaningful way the true empirical risks of the profession, because we don't have a compilation of data detailing how many dives have been attempted during the course of a given year, how long the dives lasted, and what, if any, injuries resulted. We do know, however, that the profession of commercial diving is considered a hazardous profession, because there are multiple things that could go wrong and result in injury.

Thanks to strong regulation and oversight by OSHA, the safety data submitted by reputable diving companies has reflected fewer injuries over the past decade. It's extremely difficult for a company to remain profitable if they have a poor safety record.

What makes commercial diving "hazardous" is that divers are not only working on industrial sites, which are innately hazardous, but they're also often working off moving rigs, often with very limited visibility. Add to that the fact that divers have to contend with specific maladies such as HPNS and decompression sickness. Though many commercial divers have enjoyed long healthy lives, there are unfortunately numerous ways in which you can be seriously injured or killed while performing the job. From explosions, to encounters with marine life, to drowning, the hazards are there. It's up to you to understand and avoid them.

The Buck Stops with You

If you're pursuing a career as a professional diver, then you must not be afraid to say "no" if you're asked to do something that's unsafe in your judgment. Once you're certified by the Association of Diving Contractors, you have every right to assert your judgment on safety matters, especially when it's your own personal safety that's in question. If your supervisor asks you to do something you deem unsafe, then you should simply refuse to do it, and allow the consequences to unfold as they will. If you're convinced that you're right, and you get fired for insubordination, then you may find yourself rehired as another company's safety supervisor after you tell them what happened and how you stood up for work safety. Even in a purely cynical business sense, safety is no joke.

Drowning

Though it would seem that drowning would be a major concern for commercial divers, usually drowning is not the primary cause of death for a diver. Rather, an explosion or some industrial accident that prevents the diver from being able to resurface, or causes his air supply to get damaged. For best practice, commercial divers should always wear a bailout bottle to provide a little bit more flexibility in an emergency situation. Divers are often able to survive the initial ramifications of an accident or emergency situation, but they may become delayed returning to the surface. If they can't get back up fast enough and run out of air, they will pass out and drown easily. Having the bailout bottle buys them a little more time with a bit more air.

Most injuries and deaths in the field come, not from drowning, but from complications associated with pressure, such as squeezes or differential pressure accidents.

Differential Pressure Accidents

One of the most common causes of serious injury and death among commercial divers are differential pressure accidents. A differential pressure accident refers to a situation in which a valve or dam opening isn't tested for equalized pressure before it's opened. If the pressure beyond the valve or dam opening is too low then the outside water will rush in with great ferocity. If the opening is a larger one and the pressure differential is high, then the power of the suction is enough to rip off a limb or permanently trap a diver's arm in a pipe, leading to drowning. Some accidents have resulted in the diver having his full helmet sucked off, causing him to drown.

Squeezes

A "squeeze" occurs when a pocket of air gets trapped inside the diver's body or in his suit. Because the pressure is much greater outside the air pocket than within it, a phenomenon known as a squeeze occurs, which can be fatal.

One modern tool that's helped make squeeze injuries and fatalities very rare in today's diving environment is the "non-return valve." The non-return valve, also known as the "one-way valve" prevents air from travelling the wrong way through the air hose and creating a bubble. Without this valve, a vacuum will be created that will pull strongly upwards on the diver's body in an attempt to force it into the helmet and up the hose. This is known as a squeeze and can cause injury or death.

Decompression Sickness

Even though we've already covered the basics of decompression sickness in Chapter 5, it's worth mentioning again in the context of injury avoidance. While decompression sickness is rarely fatal, an extreme shift—for example, from a deep saturated dive quickly back to normal atmospheric pressure without making the required decompression stops—can result in a fatal phenomenon called "explosive decompression."

Encounters with Marine Life

One thing that most marine divers don't tend to worry about is being attacked by a shark or other sea creature. Even though divers work in waters where sharks are present, shark attacks on commercial divers are exceedingly rare. When it comes to assaults by marine life, the worst situation commercial divers are bound to encounter are triggerfish, especially prevalent in the Gulf of Mexico. A triggerfish bite can be quite painful, though they're not likely to draw blood or cause serious injury.

In addition to the situations mentioned above, there are a multitude of other risks associated with commercial diving including standard industrial accidents and explosions. Add on the fact that divers are often required to work at odd hours for long periods of time—they're often tired and more prone to making mistakes.

Conclusion

While almost every hobbyist diver has at one point or another pondered a career in commercial diving, it's certainly not for everyone. There will be many exciting and certainly dangerous moments, along with many dull hours, especially if you're stuck on an offshore rig for weeks at a time. Divers are prone to telling stories and making up games during their down times. A lot of rigs have pool or snooker tables. There is also usually task work available to keep you busy when you're not diving, such as repairing and cleaning equipment.

Commercial diving is often an irregular gig. You're contracted out for a period of a few months, then you have a few months off. During your "on" time, you have to be ready to work for long hours every day of the week. Not everyone is cut out for it. Depending on the duration of your contract and how much money you're earning, it may be wise to have another profession help supplement your diving income when diving jobs are scarce.

Finally, I'd like to thank you for purchasing this book! If you enjoyed it or found it helpful, I'd greatly appreciate it if you'd take a moment to leave a review on Amazon. Thank you!